From Grind to Greatness:

Unleashing Your Potential and Building a Business You're Passionate About

Daniel C.Partin

Table of content

Introduction

From Grind to Greatness: Unleashing Your Potential and Building a Business You're Passionate About is a motivational and practical guide for anyone who dreams of turning their passion into a successful business.

In this book, we'll explore the journey from grinding it out in a job you don't love to building a business that aligns with your values and purpose. You'll learn the essential steps to take to unleash your potential, tap into your inner strengths, and find the courage to pursue your dreams.

Drawing on real-life examples, this book offers insightful advice on everything from finding your niche, identifying your target market, and developing a business plan to managing finances, building a brand, and marketing your products or services. You'll also gain a deeper understanding of the mindset and habits of successful entrepreneurs and how you can apply them to your own journey.

Whether you're a first-time entrepreneur or looking to take your existing business to the next level, From Grind to Greatness provides the guidance and inspiration you need to create a business that not only provides financial success but also fulfills your personal and professional goals. This book will equip you with the tools and knowledge necessary to make your business dream a reality and help you live a life of purpose and passion.

Chapter 1: Understanding Your Potential

Uncovering Your Personal Strengths

Uncovering your personal strengths is an important step in personal development. Knowing your strengths can help you to be more confident and successful in life. It can also help you to identify areas in which you need to improve and work on.

Your personal strengths are what make you unique. They are the qualities and characteristics that define you, and they are the foundation of your success. These may include qualities such as creativity, communication, analytical thinking, problem-solving, and more.

Here are some steps to help you uncover your personal strengths:

Self-Reflection: The first step to uncovering your personal strengths is to engage in self-reflection. Take some time to think about your experiences, your accomplishments, and your passions. Ask yourself questions like, "What am I good at?" "What activities bring me joy?" and "What do people often compliment me on?" You can also take personality tests or assessments to help you identify your strengths.

Seek Feedback: It's often helpful to seek feedback from others to get a better understanding of your strengths. Ask your friends, family, and colleagues to provide honest feedback on your strengths and areas where you excel. You can also consider reaching out to a coach or mentor who can provide you with more detailed feedback.

Identify Patterns: Once you have collected feedback from others, start identifying patterns in their feedback. Look for common themes that emerge and make note of them. For example, if several people have commented on your ability to communicate effectively, then communication might be a strength for you.

Experiment: Experiment with different activities and tasks to help you identify your strengths. Try new things and pay attention to activities that come naturally to you or that you find enjoyable. When you engage in activities that leverage your strengths, you are likely to feel more energized and motivated.

Practice: Once you have identified your strengths, it's important to practice and develop them. Look for opportunities to use your strengths in different areas of your life, such as work, relationships, or hobbies. Practice and repetition can help you strengthen your skills and develop greater confidence in your abilities.

Reframe Weaknesses: It's also important to reframe your weaknesses in a positive light. Rather than focusing on your weaknesses, try to focus on your strengths and how you can leverage them to overcome your weaknesses. For example, if you struggle with public speaking, focus on your strengths in written communication and prepare thoroughly for presentations.

Remember to celebrate your strengths and be proud of what you can achieve. Acknowledge your successes, and use them as motivation to keep pushing forward. With the right attitude and the right strategies, you can use your strengths to reach your goals.

Discovering Your Passion

Discovering your passion is the process of finding something that you are truly passionate about and can dedicate your time and energy to. It is a process of self-discovery, exploration, and reflection that can help you develop a clearer sense of purpose and direction in your life.

The first step to discovering your passion is to identify what makes you excited and engaged. Ask yourself what activities you enjoy doing, what topics you're most interested in, and what activities bring you the most joy. These could be anything from sports, to music, to art, to volunteering, to reading, to writing, to exploring nature. Make a list of your interests and start exploring them further.

The second step is to experiment with activities that you find interesting. Set aside time to try out different activities and see which ones you like best. Talk to others who have found success in their passions and ask them for advice. Connect with people who share your interests and find out what they are doing to pursue their passions.

The third step is to take action and pursue your passions. Once you've identified what you're passionate about, take steps to actively pursue it. Set goals and create a plan to achieve them. Research the resources and people who can help you reach your goals. Reach out to mentors who can provide guidance and support.

It's important to have patience and persevere in the face of setbacks. The process of discovering and pursuing your passions may take time, but it's worth it. Take time to reassess your goals and progress, and adjust your plans as necessary.

Discovering your passion can be a long and challenging process, but it can also be immensely rewarding. Taking the time to explore and experiment can help you uncover what drives and motivates you, and can give you the clarity and direction to pursue life goals that are meaningful to you.

Setting Goals That Align with Your Value

Setting goals that align with your values is important for achieving success. Values are the things that you hold most important.They are the foundations of your life. When you set goals based on what you value, you are more likely to take consistent action and persist through the challenging times.

The first step in setting goals that align with your values is to identify what those values are. Reflect on what you believe in and what is most important to you. Consider the people, places, and things in your life that you treasure. Write down the values that you can think of, then narrow them down to the essential few that matter most to you.

Once you have identified your values, you can use them to set meaningful goals. When you set goals, consider which of your values they reflect. For example, if you value education, you might set a goal to complete a degree. If you value family, you might set a goal to spend more time with your loved ones.

The next step is to set realistic and achievable goals. Make sure that the goals you set are specific, measurable, and attainable. Break down your goals into actionable steps and create a timeline for completion.

You should use your values to motivate you. When you have a goal that is important to you, remind yourself of why it matters. Think about how it relates to your values and how it will make a difference in your life. This will help keep you focused and motivated to achieve your goal.

Setting goals that align with your values is a powerful way to stay on track and achieve your goals. It ensures that your goals are meaningful and that you are taking action in line with what matters most to you.

Chapter 2: Building a Successful Business

Choosing a Business Model

Choosing a business model is one of the most important decisions that entrepreneurs make when starting a business. A business model is a plan that outlines how a business will generate revenue, deliver value to customers, and operate as a sustainable entity. There are many different types of business models and each has its own strengths and weaknesses.

When selecting a business model, it is important to consider the type of product or service being offered, the target market, and the resources available. The most common types of business models include product-based, service-based, subscription-based, and marketplace-based models.

Product-based models involve selling physical or digital products to customers. This could include selling physical goods such as books, clothing, or electronics, or digital goods such as software and apps. Product-based models typically require a significant upfront investment in inventory and other resources, but can be very profitable if the right products are chosen.

Service-based models involve providing a service to customers. This could include consulting, web design, or other types of services. Service-based models typically require less of an upfront investment but can be more difficult to scale.

Subscription-based models involve selling access to a product or service on a recurring basis.

This could include a monthly magazine subscription or a monthly software subscription. Subscription-based models can be very profitable if the customer base is large enough and the product or service is valued by customers.

Marketplace-based models involve connecting buyers and sellers of goods and services. This could be done through an online marketplace such as eBay or Amazon, or through a physical marketplace such as a flea market. Marketplace-based models can be very profitable if the marketplace is well-managed and there is enough demand for the products and services being sold.

In addition to the type of business model, entrepreneurs should also consider the customer base and the cost structure.

For example, if the target customers are businesses, then a product-based model may not be the most effective option. If the cost structure is too high, then the business may not be able to make a profit.

Entrepreneurs should consider the long-term sustainability of the business model. Is the model scalable? Can it be adapted to changing markets and customer needs? Will it generate enough revenue to keep the business afloat?

Choosing the right business model is essential to the success of any business. It is important to carefully consider the type of product or service being offered

Creating a Business Plan

A business plan is a formal statement of a set of business goals, the reasons why they are believed attainable, and the plan for reaching those goals. It may also contain background information about the organization or team attempting to reach those goals.

Creating a business plan is an important step in the process of starting a business. It provides direction and serves as a blueprint for the business. It allows entrepreneurs to think through their ideas, anticipate potential problems and develop strategies to overcome them. It also acts as a communication tool for attracting investors, creditors, and employees.

When creating a business plan, there are several key components that need to be considered. These include an executive summary, company description, market analysis, organization and management, service or product line, marketing and sales, funding request, financial projections, and an appendix.

The executive summary is a short overview of the business and its goals. It should provide a snapshot of the business and include key points from the other sections.

The company description should provide an overview of the company and its products or services. It should include information about the company's history, mission and values, and competitive advantages.

The market analysis should identify the industry, target market, and competitive landscape

The organization and management section should identify the organizational structure, key personnel, and management strategies.

The service or product line should provide an overview of the products or services offered. It should also include information about pricing, distribution, and product development.

The marketing and sales section should include a detailed plan for marketing and sales activities. It should include information about the target market, marketing mix, and sales strategies.

The funding request should include a request for funds and a detailed plan for how those funds will be used.

The financial projections should include financial statements and projections for the first few years of operations.

The appendix should include supporting documents such as resumes, contracts, and other relevant documents.

Creating a business plan is an important step in the process of starting a business. It provides direction and acts as a communication tool for attracting investors, creditors, and employees. By taking the time to create a comprehensive business plan, entrepreneurs can increase the chances of success for their business.

Finding Funding and Investors

Finding funding and investors can be a daunting task for entrepreneurs and small business owners. It requires time, effort and research, but it can be done.

When seeking funding and investors, the first step is to create a business plan. This should include an executive summary, industry and competitive analysis, product and market forecast, company financials, and marketing strategy. A well-crafted business plan will help attract potential investors and showcase the value of the business.

Another important step is to network. Attending conferences, industry events, and other networking opportunities can help entrepreneurs to meet potential investors and build relationships. Additionally, entrepreneurs should use social media to network, advertise their business, and build an online presence.

Once potential investors are identified, entrepreneurs must present their business plans and explain why their company is worth investing in. Presentations should be professional and provide relevant statistical data and market trends.

Once an investor has been identified, entrepreneurs should be prepared to negotiate the terms of the investment. This includes the amount of the investment, the ownership stake and voting rights, and the timeline for repayment.

Entrepreneurs should be aware of the various sources of funding available. These include venture capital, angel investors, crowdfunding, government grants, and loans from banks or other financial institutions. Each of these sources has different requirements and expectations, so it is important to do research and understand the details before pursuing any particular option.

Ultimately, finding funding and investors requires research, networking, and negotiation. It is a process that requires time and effort, but can be very rewarding for entrepreneurs who are able to successfully secure the necessary investments to grow their businesses.

Hiring the Right People

Hiring the right people is essential to any organization's success. People are the most valuable asset of any company, and getting the right fit for any position can mean the difference between success and failure. The right hire can bring enthusiasm, dedication, and a wealth of knowledge to a team, while the wrong hire can cause a great deal of disruption and damage.

When it comes to hiring the right people, the first step is to develop a clear job description. This should outline the duties, responsibilities, and qualifications for the role in question. It should also define the organizational culture and values that an applicant will be expected to embody. This will help to ensure that applicants have a good understanding of what is expected of them and will help to narrow down the pool of applicants.

The next step is to create a comprehensive recruitment strategy. This should include advertising the role and recruiting through social media, job boards, and other online platforms. It should also include actively seeking out suitable candidates through networking and referrals.

Once a suitable pool of applicants has been identified, it is important to screen each candidate thoroughly. This can include conducting background checks, interviewing and testing, and reviewing references. This will help to ensure that the most suitable candidate is selected for the role.

It is important to provide a comprehensive onboarding process for new hires. This should include training and development, a clear job description, and an understanding of the organizational culture and values. This will help to ensure that new hires have a good understanding of their role and have the necessary skills and knowledge to be successful in their new role.

Hiring the right people is essential for any organization's success. It is important to develop a comprehensive recruitment strategy, screen applicants carefully, and provide a comprehensive onboarding process for new hires. Doing so will help to ensure that the most suitable candidates are selected and that new hires have the necessary skills and knowledge to succeed.

Marketing Your Business

Marketing your business is an essential part of operating a successful business. It is a way to reach out to potential customers and inform them of the products or services you offer. It is a way to establish a connection with your customers, build relationships, and create a positive brand image. Marketing your business can also help you to stay competitive in the market and increase your profits.

The first step in marketing your business is to create a marketing plan. This plan should include your target audience, the types of marketing strategies you will use, and the budget for your marketing efforts. It is important to consider the different types of marketing that would work best for your business, such as online marketing or traditional marketing.

Online marketing is a type of marketing that utilizes the internet and digital technologies to reach customers. This includes email marketing, content marketing, search engine optimization, social media marketing, and more. It is used to create relationships with potential customers, promote products and services, and drive sales. It can be used to reach local, national, or international audiences.

Traditional marketing refers to the use of traditional advertising methods to reach potential customers. These methods have been in use for many years and include tactics such as print advertising, TV and radio commercials, direct mail, billboards, and telemarketing.

Once you have created a marketing plan, the next step is to develop a brand identity. This includes creating a logo, developing a tagline, and other branding elements. Branding will help you to create recognition and distinguish your business from others in the market.

Another important step in marketing your business is to promote your products and services. You can do this through various methods such as advertising, direct mail, public relations, search engine optimization, and social media. It is important to choose the right channels to reach your target audience.

Advertising,: it is a form of marketing that involves creating an awareness of a product or service. Advertising can be done through radio, television, print, online, and other media. The goal of advertising is to create a positive perception of the product or service and to persuade consumers to purchase it.

Public relations: It involves creating relationships with customers, stakeholders, influencers, and the media. Public relations activities can include press releases, interviews, events, and more. The goal of public relations is to create a positive image of the company and its products or services.

Digital marketing: It is a form of marketing that is done through digital channels such as search engines, social media, and websites. Digital marketing activities can include SEO, content marketing, email marketing, and more. The goal of digital marketing is to reach customers and promote products or services.

Direct mail: It is a form of marketing that involves sending physical mail to customers. Direct mail can be used to promote products or services, inform customers about special offers, or provide information about upcoming events. The goal of direct mail is to create an awareness of the product or service and to persuade customers to purchase it

It is important to measure the results of your marketing efforts. This can be done through tracking website analytics, conducting customer surveys, and monitoring customer feedback. This will help you identify areas of improvement and determine which strategies are most effective.

Marketing your business is an important part of operating a successful business. It can help you reach out to potential customers, build relationships, create recognition, and increase your profits. With the right plan and the right strategies, you can ensure your business is successful.

Growing Your Bussiness

Growing your business is an important step in ensuring that your business is successful and profitable. It involves expanding your customer base, increasing revenue, and improving your products and services. There are a number of steps you can take to grow your business, such as developing a focused business plan, identifying target markets, increasing marketing efforts, and leveraging technology.

1. Develop a Focused Business Plan: A focused business plan is essential for any business that wants to grow. A business plan will help you identify your goals and objectives, as well as map out strategies for achieving them. It should include a market analysis to determine your target market, a competitive analysis to determine how you can stand out from competitors, and a financial analysis to help you budget for growth.

2. Identify Target Markets: It's important to identify target markets to ensure that you reach the right customers. Target markets can be identified through market research, surveys, and customer feedback. Once identified, you can tailor your marketing efforts and products/services to meet their needs.

3. Increase Marketing Efforts: It's important to increase your marketing efforts to reach new customers. This can include developing a website, utilizing social media, and investing in digital marketing. You should

also consider traditional marketing tactics such as direct mail, print advertising, and radio/TV.

4. Leverage Technology: Leveraging technology is an important step in growing your business. Investing in the right technology can help you streamline processes, increase efficiency, and reduce costs. Additionally, it can help you reach a broader audience and provide better customer service.

5. Network: Building relationships with contacts in your industry is a great way to grow your business. Networking can open up opportunities for partnerships, collaborations, and referrals. You should also consider attending conferences and events to meet potential customers and partners.

These are just a few steps you can take to grow your business. It's important to stay focused and take consistent action to ensure success. With the right plan and effort, you can make your business more successful and profitable.

Chapter 3 :Developing Your Leadership Skill

Building a Strong Team

A strong team is essential for any organization to be successful. A strong team is one that works together, communicates effectively, and is able to achieve the desired results. Building a strong team takes time and effort, but the results are worth it. Here are some key steps to follow when building a strong team:

1. Establish Clear Goals: Before building a team, it is important to identify the team's purpose and objectives. This helps to ensure that everyone is working towards the same goal and all team members understand the importance of the task at hand.

2. Select the Right Members: Selecting the right members for a team is essential. It is important to have team members who have the right skills and abilities to complete the tasks. It is also important to select members who have the right attitude and will be able to contribute to the team dynamics.

3. Foster Communication: Communication is key to any successful team. It is important to create an environment where team members feel comfortable to communicate and share ideas. This helps to ensure that everyone is on the same page and can work together effectively.

4. Encourage Collaboration: Encourage team members to collaborate and work together. By working together, team members can learn from each other and be more productive.

5. Recognize and Reward: Recognizing and rewarding team members for their contributions helps to motivate them and will make them more likely to stay with the team.

6. Adapt to Change: Change is inevitable, and it is important to be able to adapt to changing circumstances. This will help the team to remain flexible and able to respond quickly to any new challenges that may arise.

Building a strong team is essential for any organization to be successful. Implementing the steps outlined above will help to ensure that the team is successful and can achieve its goals.

Developing Effective Communication Skills

Effective communication skills are essential for success in almost all aspects of life. They are particularly important in the workplace where they can help to foster better working relationships, increase productivity and ensure that everyone is on the same page.

Developing effective communication skills is a process that takes time and effort. It involves understanding the fundamentals of effective communication, such as body language, active listening, and non-verbal cues, as well as learning how to use different methods of communication, such as writing, speaking, and presenting.

The first step in developing effective communication skills is to become aware of your own communication style. Are you a passive communicator who tends to let others take the lead, or an assertive speaker who takes charge of the conversation?

Once you have identified your style, you can start to make changes to improve your communication skills. Work on being a better listener by paying attention to what the other person is saying and responding accordingly. Learn to ask questions and give feedback in a constructive way.

Another important part of effective communication is being able to read non-verbal cues. Pay attention to body language and other non-verbal cues in order to better understand what the other person is trying to communicate.

In addition to verbal and nonverbal communication, you can also use writing to express yourself. Writing can be an effective way to communicate with others, especially when you need to take the time to think through and organize your thoughts.

Consider taking a course or attending a workshop on communication skills. These courses can help you learn the basics of communication, practice your skills, and receive feedback from an experienced instructor.

Developing effective communication skills takes time and effort, but the rewards are well worth the effort. With improved communication skills, you can build better relationships, increase productivity, and better understand the people around you.

Remember, effective communication is a two-way street. You must be willing to listen and understand the other person in order to be an effective communicator.

With practice and perseverance, you can become a better communicator and achieve greater success in all areas of your life.

Managing Conflict and Difficult Conversations

Managing conflict and difficult conversations is an important skill for any leader or manager. Conflict is a natural part of any professional and personal relationship, and it is important to learn how to effectively manage it and have productive conversations.

The first step in managing conflict is to identify the source of the conflict. Once the source of the conflict is identified, it is important to understand how both parties are feeling and thinking. This can be done by asking questions, listening carefully to each other, and really understanding the other person's perspective. It is also important to maintain a positive attitude and to remain open to different perspectives.

Once the source of the conflict has been identified, it is important to create a plan for resolving the conflict. This can be done by brainstorming solutions, understanding the interests of both parties, and identifying potential solutions. It is also important to create a safe and respectful environment for both parties to discuss the conflict.

It is also important to be prepared for difficult conversations. This can be done by preparing for the conversation by gathering relevant data, considering alternative solutions, and having a plan for the conversation. It is also important to maintain a respectful attitude, be patient, and listen carefully to the other person.

It is important to remember that different people have different perspectives, and it is important to be open to different ways of addressing the conflict or conversation. It is also important to remember that conflict does not always need to be solved, but can be managed and the parties can work together to reach a resolution.

By understanding how to manage conflict and have difficult conversations, leaders and managers can create an environment of understanding and collaboration. This can help to foster a productive and positive work environment.

Making Decisions That Keep Your Team Motivated

Making decisions that keep your team motivated can be a challenging process. It requires careful consideration of the team's goals, objectives and resources. To ensure success, leaders should create an environment where everyone feels heard, respected and valued. Additionally, they must be willing to take risks, be flexible, and maintain a positive attitude.

When making decisions, leaders should take into account their team's needs and desires. This means listening to the team and allowing them to express their opinions. Leaders should also consider the team's strengths and weaknesses, and use these to guide their decisions. When possible, give team members autonomy and the freedom to make their own decisions. This will help to keep them engaged and motivated.

Leaders should also consider how their decisions will affect the team. Will their decision help to achieve the team's goals? Will it create new opportunities for growth? How will it affect team morale? Making sure to consider these factors will help to ensure that decisions are made in the best interests of the team.

Leaders should be willing to take risks. Making decisions without taking risks is rarely effective. Taking risks can open up new opportunities and help the team to grow. However, it is important to ensure that the risks are calculated and that the team is prepared to handle them.

Making decisions that keep your team motivated requires careful consideration of the team's goals, objectives and resources.

Leaders should create an environment where everyone feels heard and respected, be willing to take risks and be flexible, and consider how their decisions will affect the team. Doing so will help to ensure that decisions are made in the best interests of the team and that the team remains motivated.

Chapter 4: Navigating Challenges

Managing Risk and Uncertainty

Managing risk and uncertainty is an essential aspect of any successful business strategy. Risk refers to the potential loss that a business may experience due to internal or external factors, while uncertainty refers to the inability to predict future events with complete accuracy.

To manage risk and uncertainty effectively, businesses need to take a proactive approach and implement risk management strategies. Here are some steps that businesses can take to manage risk and uncertainty:

Identify and Assess Risks: The first step is to identify and assess the risks that may affect the business. This can be done by conducting a risk assessment, which involves identifying potential risks and assessing their likelihood and potential impact on the business.

Develop a Risk Management Plan: Once the risks have been identified and assessed, a risk management plan should be developed. This plan should include strategies to mitigate or avoid the risks, as well as contingency plans in case the risks cannot be completely avoided.

Implement the Plan: The risk management plan should be implemented across the organization, and all employees should be trained on how to manage risk and uncertainty effectively. This may involve implementing new policies, procedures, or technologies to mitigate risks.

Monitor and Review: The risk management plan should be monitored and reviewed regularly to ensure that it remains effective and relevant. This may involve conducting regular risk assessments, reviewing the effectiveness of risk management strategies, and making adjustments to the plan as needed.

Maintain a Culture of Risk Awareness: Finally, businesses should maintain a culture of risk awareness throughout the organization. This means that employees should be encouraged to identify and report potential risks, and that risk management should be integrated into all aspects of the business.

Overall, managing risk and uncertainty requires a proactive and ongoing approach. By identifying and assessing risks, developing a risk management plan, implementing the plan, monitoring and reviewing progress, and maintaining a culture of risk awareness, businesses can effectively manage risk and uncertainty and minimize the potential impact on their operations.

Dealing with Setbacks

Setbacks are a natural part of life and can be difficult to deal with. However, they are also an opportunity for growth and development. Here are some strategies for dealing with setbacks:

Recognize and acknowledge the setback: The first step in dealing with setbacks is to recognize and acknowledge them. It's important to accept that setbacks happen and that they are a natural part of life.

Take time to process your emotions: It's normal to feel upset, angry, or frustrated when faced with a setback. Take time to process your emotions and allow yourself to feel them fully. This can help you move past them more quickly.

Evaluate what went wrong: Once you have processed your emotions, take some time to evaluate what went wrong. This can help you identify areas where you need to improve and can help you avoid making the same mistake in the future.

Learn from the setback: Setbacks can be a valuable learning experience. Take the opportunity to learn from your setback and use what you have learned to grow and develop.

Focus on the positives: It's easy to get caught up in the negatives when faced with a setback. However, it's important to focus on the positives as well. Think about what you have accomplished and what you are grateful for.

Develop a plan for moving forward: Once you have evaluated the setback and learned from it, develop a plan for moving forward. This plan should include specific actions you can take to overcome the setback and achieve your goals.

Take action: The final step in dealing with setbacks is to take action. Put your plan into action and work towards overcoming the setback. Remember that setbacks are a natural part of life, and it's how you respond to them that determines your success.

Setbacks can be difficult to deal with, but they are also an opportunity for growth and development. By recognizing and acknowledging setbacks, processing your emotions, evaluating what went wrong, learning from the setback, focusing on the positives, developing a plan for moving forward, and taking action, you can overcome setbacks and achieve your goals.

Maintaining Your Mental Health and Well-Being

Maintaining good mental health and well-being is essential for living a happy, fulfilling life. In today's fast-paced and stressful world, it can be challenging to prioritize self-care, but taking care of your mental health is just as important as taking care of your physical health. Here are some tips for maintaining your mental health and well-being:

Practice mindfulness and meditation: Mindfulness and meditation can help reduce stress and anxiety and increase feelings of calmness and relaxation. Try setting aside a few minutes each day to meditate or practice mindfulness.

Stay active: Exercise has been shown to have numerous mental health benefits, including reducing symptoms of depression and anxiety and improving mood. Find an activity you enjoy and make it a regular part of your routine.

Connect with others: Social support is important for mental health and well-being. Make an effort to connect with friends and family regularly, join a club or group with similar interests, or volunteer in your community.

Prioritize self-care: Take time for yourself each day to do something you enjoy, whether it's reading, taking a bath, or practicing a hobby. Prioritizing self-care can help reduce stress and improve your overall mood.

Eat a healthy diet: Eating a well-balanced diet can help improve mood and reduce symptoms of depression and anxiety. Focus on eating whole, nutrient-dense foods and limiting processed foods and sugar.

Get enough sleep: Sleep plays a crucial role in mental health and well-being. Aim for 7-8 hours of sleep each night and establish a consistent sleep routine.

Practice gratitude: Focusing on the positive aspects of your life and expressing gratitude can help improve your overall mood and reduce feelings of stress and anxiety. Try writing down three things you're grateful for each day.

Seek professional help if needed: If you're struggling with your mental health, don't hesitate to seek professional help. A therapist or counselor can help you develop coping skills and strategies for managing stress and improving your mental health.

Maintaining good mental health and well-being requires a holistic approach that includes self-care, social support, healthy habits, and professional help when needed. By prioritizing your mental health and taking steps to care for yourself, you can improve your overall well-being and enjoy a happier, more fulfilling life.

Conclusion

From grind to greatness is a journey that requires a great deal of effort, commitment, and determination. It involves pushing through challenges, overcoming obstacles, and staying focused on one's goals. Whether it is in business, sports, or personal growth, the path from grind to greatness is not an easy one, but those who are willing to put in the work can achieve tremendous success and fulfillment.

One of the key ingredients for success on this journey is hard work. Whether it's in the form of consistent practice, tireless effort, or a willingness to put in long hours, hard work is what allows individuals to make progress and achieve their goals. It requires a strong work ethic, a willingness to put in the effort even when it's difficult, and a refusal to give up in the face of setbacks and failures.

Another important element of the journey from grind to greatness is discipline. This involves developing good habits and routines that help individuals stay focused and on track. It requires setting clear goals and priorities, and making choices that align with those goals. Discipline also involves making sacrifices, saying no to distractions and temptations that can derail progress, and staying committed to the task at hand.

Preserverance is critical on the path from grind to greatness. This involves staying the course even when progress seems slow or setbacks occur. It requires a willingness to learn from failures, adapt to new situations, and keep moving forward. Perseverance means maintaining a positive attitude and mindset, even in the face of adversity.

The journey from grind to greatness requires a combination of hard work, discipline, and perseverance. It is not an easy path, but those who are willing to put in the effort can achieve tremendous success and fulfillment. By staying committed to their goals, remaining focused on the task at hand, and pushing through the tough times, individuals can transform a grind into greatness and achieve their full potential.

www.ingramcontent.com/pod-product-compliance
Lightning Source LLC
Chambersburg PA
CBHW070849220526
45466CB00005B/1948